First Facts

Your
Body
Syst

Your
Digestive

System
Works!

by Flora Brett

CAPSTONE PRESS
a capstone imprint

First Facts are published by Capstone Press,
1710 Roe Crest Drive, North Mankato, Minnesota 56003
www.capstonepub.com

Library of Congress Cataloging-in-Publication Data
Brett, Flora, author.
Your digestive system works! / by Flora Brett.
    pages cm. — (First facts. Your body systems)
Summary: "Engaging text and informative images help readers learn about their digestive
system."— Provided by publisher.
Audience: Ages 6–9.
Audience: K to grade 3.
Includes bibliographical references and index.
ISBN 978-1-4914-2064-5 (library binding) — ISBN 978-1-4914-2248-9 (pbk.) —
ISBN 978-1-4914-2270-0 (ebook PDF)
1. Digestion—Juvenile literature. 2. Digestive organs—Juvenile literature. 3. Human
physiology—Juvenile literature. I. Title.
QP145.B64 2015
612.3—dc23   2014023830

Editorial Credits
Emily Raij and Nikki Bruno Clapper, editors; Cynthia Akiyoshi, designer;
Svetlana Zhurkin, media researcher; Laura Manthe, production specialist

Photo Credits
Shutterstock: AntiMartina (dotted background), cover and throughout, Blamb, 21, Bo Valentino,
20, decade3d, 1, 13, 19, Leonello Calvetti, 5, mikeledray, 9, Monkey Business Images, 7,
Sebastian Kaulitzki, cover, 11, Thomas M. Perkins, cover (top right), back cover, 1 (top right),
Vladislav Kozorez, 15; SuperStock: Science Picture Co, 17

Printed in the United States of America in North Mankato, Minnesota.
092014   008482CGS15

Table of Contents

Food on the Move

The smell of baking bread is in the air. Your mouth begins to water. Even before you take a bite, your digestive system starts working. The digestive system helps your body get **nutrients** and energy from food. Everything you eat travels 30 feet (9 meters) through your digestive tract. This journey is called **digestion**.

nutrient—something that is needed by people, animals, and plants to stay healthy and strong

digestion—the process a body uses to turn food into energy

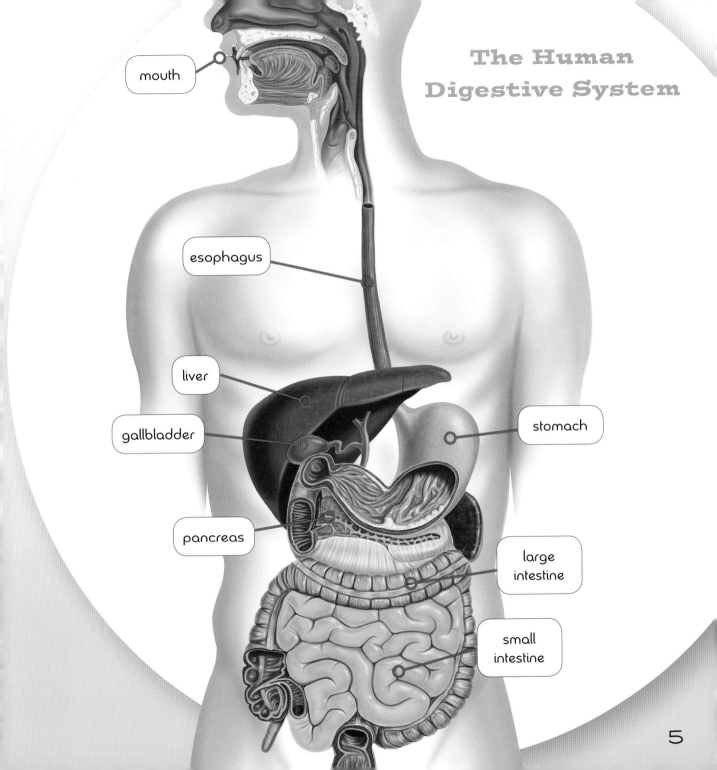

The Human Digestive System

mouth

esophagus

liver

gallbladder

pancreas

stomach

large intestine

small intestine

Getting Nutrients

Digestion starts with your teeth and ends when waste leaves your body. During digestion, your body breaks down food. It also takes in nutrients from what you eat and drink.

Your body needs nutrients to stay healthy. Nutrients like water, carbohydrates, fats, proteins, minerals, and vitamins give your body energy. Energy helps you run, talk, think, breathe, and grow.

Fact:

Water is a very important nutrient. About 60 percent of the human body is made up of water!

The Mouth

Digestion begins with the mouth. Your front teeth bite into an apple. Your back teeth grind the apple into smaller pieces. Your brain tells your glands to send in a rush of saliva. Saliva makes the food soft and wet. Enzymes in your saliva break down the apple more.

Once the apple is mushy, you can swallow it. Your tongue rolls the chewed apple into a ball that is easy to swallow.

gland—an organ in the body that makes natural chemicals or helps substances leave the body

saliva—the clear liquid in your mouth that helps you swallow and begin to digest food

enzyme—a substance that helps break down food

Fact:

Your taste buds tell you what food tastes like and what's safe to eat. But food needs to mix with saliva before taste buds start working.

9

The Upper Digestive Tract

Swallowed food travels into the upper digestive tract. This tract includes the throat, the **esophagus**, and the stomach.

Food travels 10 inches (25 centimeters) down the esophagus. Muscles in the esophagus move food the way fingers squeeze toothpaste from a tube. Another ring of muscles lies at the end of the esophagus. These muscles control how much food enters the stomach.

esophagus—the tube that carries food from the mouth to the stomach; muscles in the esophagus push food into the stomach

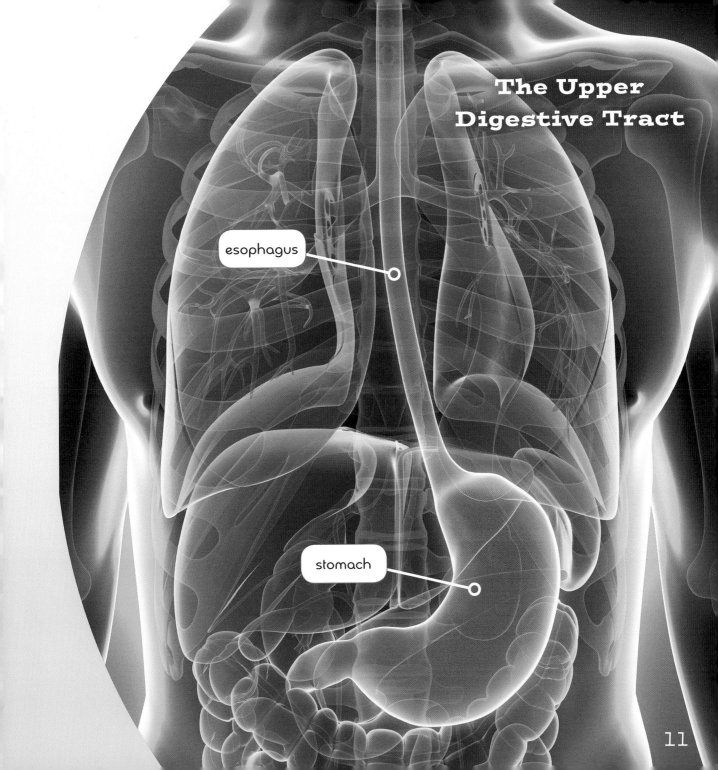

The Upper Digestive Tract

esophagus

stomach

The Stomach

The stomach is a stretchy pouch below the esophagus. Food stays there for about three hours. During this time, the stomach's powerful muscles churn the food.

The stomach adds acid and other liquids to food. These materials break down food into a soupy mixture. They also kill bacteria. A layer of mucus protects stomach walls from the strong acid.

Fact:

Sea horses and platypuses do not have stomachs. Their food goes straight from the esophagus to the intestines.

acid—a strong liquid; stomach acids help break down food for energy

bacteria—very small living things that exist all around you and inside you; some bacteria cause disease

mucus—a sticky or slimy fluid that coats and protects the inside of the stomach

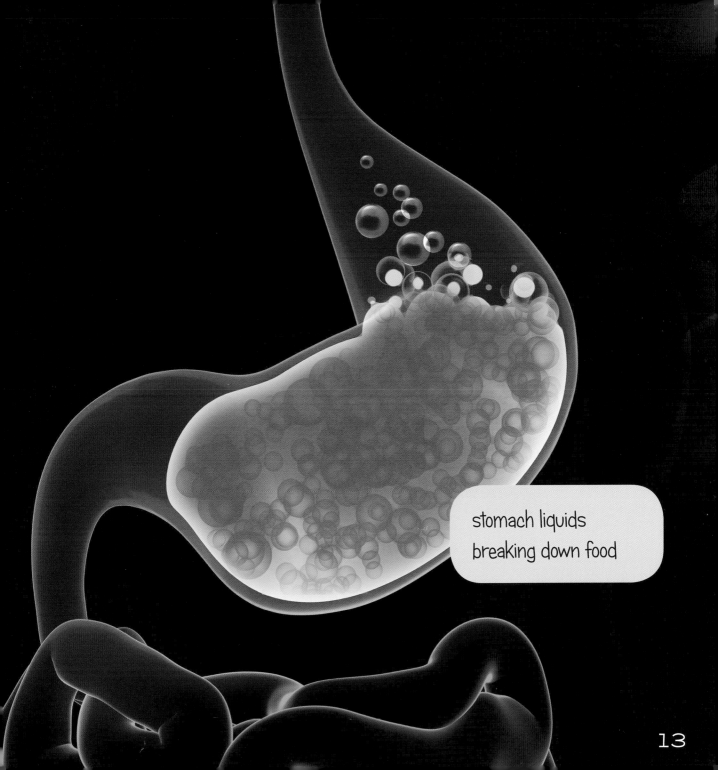

stomach liquids
breaking down food

13

The Lower Digestive Tract

The soupy food then moves into the small intestine. This body part is coiled tightly under your stomach. Nutrients from food pass through the organ's walls and into the blood.

Next, food moves into the large intestine. The large intestine is wider but shorter than the small intestine. The large intestine absorbs water and collects the parts of food the body can't use. The body gets rid of this waste as poop.

Fact:

The small intestine is the longest part of the digestive system. Stretched out, it is about 22 feet (7 meters) long.

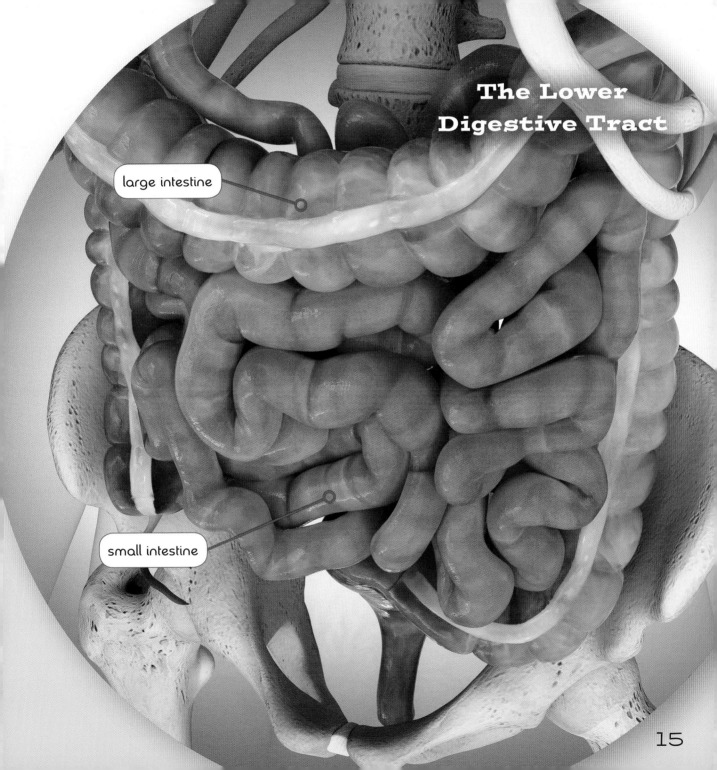

The Lower Digestive Tract

large intestine

small intestine

Digestion and Circulation

Organs called the pancreas, liver, and gallbladder send juices to the small intestine. These juices break down nutrients from food. Millions of fingerlike **villi** soak up the nutrients.

The **circulatory system** and the digestive system work together to move nutrients through the body. Tiny **blood vessels** pick up nutrients from the villi. Blood carries the nutrients to the rest of the body.

villi—tiny parts of the small intestine that soak up nutrients

circulatory system—the system that moves blood throughout your body

blood vessel—a narrow tube that carries blood through your body

Fact:
Many people believe that most digestion happens in the stomach. Actually, most digestion happens in the small intestine.

villi

Where Does the Waste Go?

Waste passes through a part of the large intestine called the **colon**. The colon absorbs any remaining water and harmful substances. The waste hardens and becomes solid poop.

Then the waste is pushed into the **rectum**. This is the digestive tract's last stop. Waste stays in the rectum until you go to the bathroom.

colon—part of the large intestine that absorbs water and harmful chemicals from waste and pushes waste to the rectum

rectum—the final, straight part of the large intestine

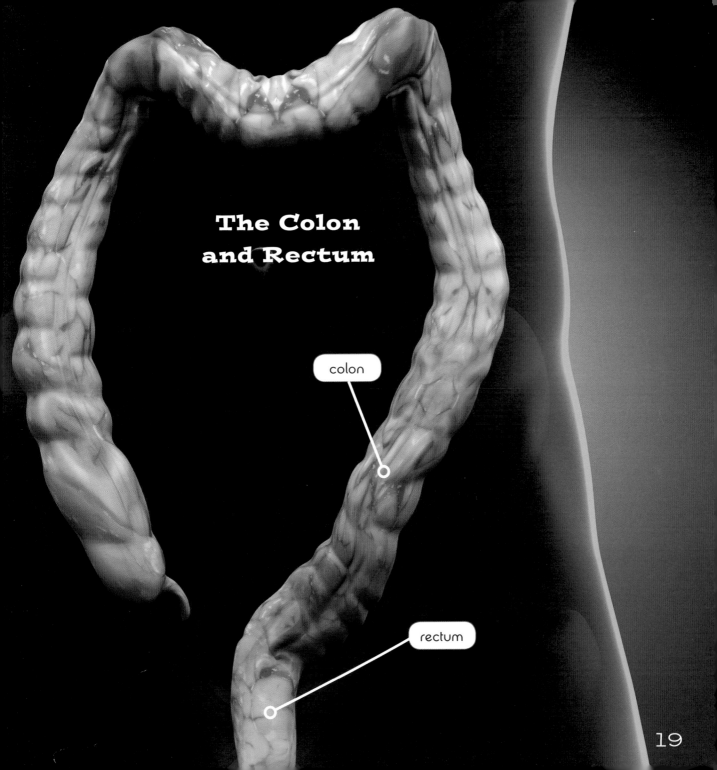

The Colon and Rectum

colon

rectum

Digestive Problems

Germs from spoiled, dirty, or poorly cooked food can cause digestive problems. Your body gets rid of germs by throwing up or having diarrhea.

The digestive system keeps your body going. It makes sure you get nutrients and keeps germs out. It is truly an amazing body system.

Fact:

Some foods, like corn and carrots, are difficult for the body to digest. That's why your poop may have whole pieces of food in it.

Amazing but True!

Have you ever had something "go down the wrong pipe"? That means the drink went down your windpipe instead of your esophagus. A flap in the back of your throat usually blocks liquid from your windpipe. But sometimes the flap doesn't have time to close. Then you cough to clear your windpipe.

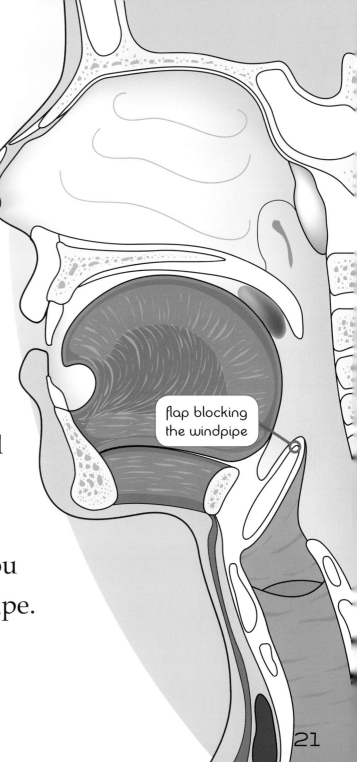

flap blocking the windpipe

21

Glossary

acid (ASS-id)—a strong liquid; acids help break down food for energy

bacteria (bak-TEER-ee-uh)—very small living things that exist all around you and inside you; some bacteria cause disease

blood vessel (BLUHD VE-suhl)—a narrow tube that carries blood through your body

circulatory system (SIR-kyuh-luh-tor-ee SIS-tuhm)—the system that moves blood throughout your body

colon (KOH-lun)—part of the large intestine that absorbs water and harmful chemicals from waste and pushes waste to the rectum

digestion (dye-JESS-chuhn)—the process a body uses to turn food into energy

enzyme (EN-zime)—a substance that helps break down food

esophagus (e-SOF-uh-guhss)—the tube that carries food from the mouth to the stomach; muscles in the esophagus push food into the stomach

gland (GLAND)—an organ in the body that makes natural chemicals or helps substances leave the body

mucus (MYOO-kuhss)—a sticky or slimy fluid that coats and protects the inside of the stomach

nutrient (NOO-tree-uhnt)—something that is needed by people, animals, and plants to stay healthy and strong

rectum (REK-tum)—the final, straight part of the large intestine

saliva (suh-LYE-vuh)—the clear liquid in your mouth that helps you swallow and begin to digest food

villi (VIH-lye)—tiny parts of the small intestine that soak up nutrients

Read More

Gray, Susan H. *The Digestive System*. Mankato, Minn.: Childs World, 2014.

Guillain, Charlotte. *Our Stomachs*. Our Bodies. Chicago: Heinemann Library, 2010.

Kolpin, Molly. *A Tour of Your Digestive System.* First Graphics: Body Systems. North Mankato, Minn.: Capstone Press, 2013.

Internet Sites

FactHound offers a safe, fun way to find Internet sites related to this book. All of the sites on FactHound have been researched by our staff.

Here's all you do:
Visit *www.facthound.com*
Type in this code: 9781491420645

Check out projects, games and lots more at
www.capstonekids.com

Critical Thinking
Using the Common Core

1. How do parts of your digestive system work to remove bacteria from your body? (Key Ideas and Details)

2. Think about a time when you got a stomachache after eating. How could you keep your digestive system free from germs in the future? (Integration of Knowledge and Ideas)

3. Explain how the digestive system works with the circulatory system to move nutrients throughout the body. (Key Ideas and Details)

Index